WWF* OFFICIAL ANNUAL

Contents

Publisher & Editor-in-Chief: **Thomas H.W. Emanuel** • Executive Editor: **Edward R. Ricciuti** • Staff Writer: **Lou Gianfriddo** • Design: **JAT Associates** • Photography Director: **Stephen H. Taylor** • Staff Photographer: **Tom Buchanan** • Production Director: **Alina L. Massaro** • Photo Editors: **Marybeth Marrion, Suzanne Pullen** • Copy Editor: **Midge Bacon** • Typesetting Manager: **Linda L. Nishball** • Puzzles: **Larry Humber** • Special thanks to: **Renée Fortin, Matt Kornhaas** • Illustration: **Scott Fisher**.

Published by Grandreams Limited, Jadwin House, 205/211 Kentish Town Road, London, NW5 2JU
Printed in Belgium. ISBN 0 86227 908 9

£4.50

HULK HOGAN

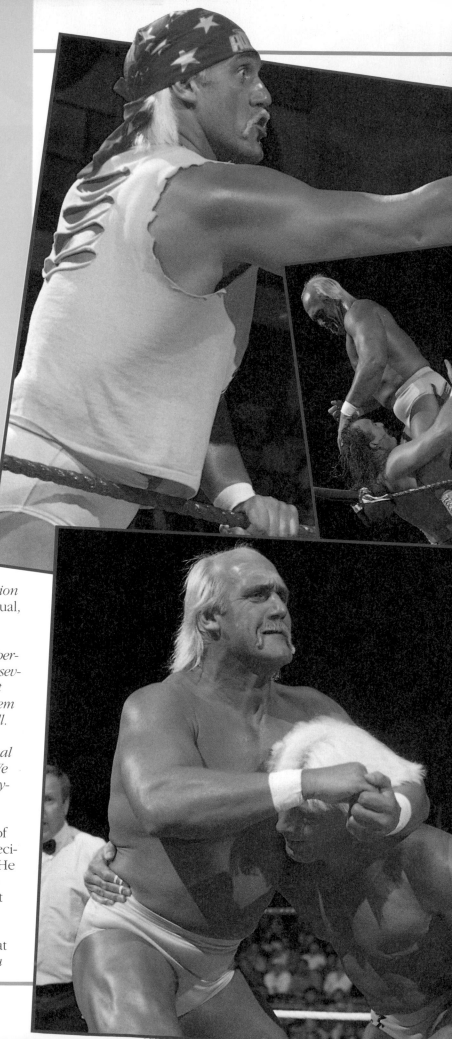

This is the second edition of the WWF Official Annual, especially for fans in the United Kingdom. World Wrestling Federation Superstars have visited the UK several times within the past year, and you will see them there in the future as well. The UK is now "WWF Country," and this annual is available only there. We hope it adds to your enjoyment of WWF events.

Hulk Hogan made one of the most monumental decisions in his life in 1992. He decided that his *WrestleMania VIII* match against Sid Justice would be his last in the WWF. At the same time, he vowed that the spirit of *Hulkamania*

would never die, and he pledged eternal loyalty to the fans who supported—and still support—him.

The year was also an eventful one for the Hulk-ster in other ways. At the *Survivor Series*, he lost his WWF Championship to the Undertaker due to interference with a chair by Ric Flair. Six days later he took it back from the Undertaker, in a match mandated by WWF President Jack Tunney. In that match, Flair again interfered with a chair, and a brawl ensued. Tunney was caught in it and knocked cold. After coming around,

a groggy Tunney knew that
the Hulkster had pinned the
Undertaker but, remember-
ing a chair was involved,
declared the title vacant.
The new champion would
be the winner of the 30-
man *Royal Rumble* in Janu-
ary. The Hulkster came
close to winning. However,
Flair, using endurance, guile
and wrestling skill, emerged
the champion. At *Wrestle-
Mania VIII* Hogan won by
disqualification over Sid
Justice after Papa Shango
joined Sid in attacking the
Hulkster. Hogan was saved
by the surprise entry of the
Ultimate Warrior.

MACHO MAN RANDY SAVAGE*

What a year for the Macho Man! At *SummerSlam*, he and Elizabeth were married. But Jake "The Snake" Roberts appeared at their wedding reception and terrorized Elizabeth with a cobra. Later, he jumped Savage and allowed a king cobra to bite him.

Trouble continued for Savage and his bride when *WWF Magazine* published photos allegedly showing Elizabeth with Ric Flair

before she met the Macho Man. Flair, it turned out, had doctored the photos, making it appear as if he had been with Elizabeth. Randy, wild with rage, took it to the ring when he met Flair at *WrestleMania VIII*. "It's gonna be just you and the Macho Man," Savage threatened Flair before the match. "And then it's just gonna be the Macho Man." Savage waged a tumultous battle against Flair and won.

THE UNDERTAKER*

The Undertaker can claim that he held the WWF Title, but only for less than a week. True, he beat Hulk Hogan, with more than a little help from Ric Flair. Then Hogan whipped him, but the title was quickly vacated by WWF President Jack Tunney pending the outcome of the *Royal Rumble*.

After the title loss, there were changes in this terrifying titan. He had walked dark ways with Jake "The Snake" Roberts. But Jake went so far in terrorizing Elizabeth, bride of Randy Savage, that it disgusted the Undertaker. He intercepted a Snake ambush attempt on Savage and Elizabeth.

The Snake struck back and attacked the Undertaker on *The Funeral Parlor*, hosted by the Undertaker's manager, Paul Bearer. Jake was lucky to get away with his skin. But at *WrestleMania VIII*, the Undertaker got hold of Jake and gave him a beating he'll remember.

Flying through the air with the greatest of ease, prepare to meet the world's finest

To succeed in the WWF, many superstars employ aerial maneuvers in their arsenals. They do so, they say, because it enables them to keep the opposition off-balance and —in some instances—to set them up for a finisher of aerial design. WWF commentator and former wrestler Gorilla

Monsoon has watched the WWF aerial age evolve.

"While I was wrestling, not too many guys were executing dropkicks or high cross-bodyblocks," says Monsoon. "Now every superstar uses some sort of aerial tactic."

Monsoon has a point. A quick glance at the WWF's talent roster says it all.

Take El Matador, for instance. He utilizes the air with great efficiency. His signature tactic, "el passeo del muerte," involving a flying forearm to the base of the skull, has secured him many victories.

From time to time, Mr. Fuji's massive Berzerker also uses the air to inflict punishment. He pulverizes foes with big legdrops off the ropes before hurling them to the arena floor.

It's also awesome when Macho Man Randy Savage soars through the air. A known aerialist, Savage has one of the best aerial attacks in the WWF. His favorite tactic, the elbow from the top ropes, has garnered Savage countless wins and several titles, including a WWF Title.

The Rocket Owen Hart is another super aerialist. He dazzles opponents with flying crescent kicks off the ropes and moonsaults from the top turnbuckles. He polishes off his adversaries with a big splash called the Rocket Launcher from the top corner pads.

WWF Tag Team co-titlist Million Dollar Man Ted

DiBiase frequently utilizes an airborne assault. His flying powerslams off the ropes are second to none.

Rowdy Roddy Piper also mixes aerial maneuvers into his arsenal. He does so, he says, in order to throw his opponents off-balance. Usually, he strikes with punches from the second turnbuckle.

Hawk and Animal, the Legion of Doom, use the aerial, extremely deadly Doomsday Device clothesline to render their opponents combat-ineffective.

Many other WWF stars besides those mentioned here employ aerial maneuvers. These high-fliers of the WWF add an exciting dimension to the battles within the squared circle.

Aerialists!

RIC FLAIR *

He said he'd do it, and he did. Ric Flair was the last man in the ring at the 1992 *Royal Rumble*—and that meant he was the new WWF Champion. Wrestlers enter the *Royal Rumble* in sequence by luck of the draw. Flair hit the ring third. Going in that early and staying until victory was an unheard-of achievement in the *Rumble*. But Flair managed it. "Like it, don't like it," Flair sneered. "You've got to live with it."

Flair won by combining craft, guts, brawling and scientific wrestling. He hid out when he had to and fought whenever it was necessary. Whether you like him or not, it was amazing.

But so was Macho Man Randy Savage, who wrestled Flair in a *WrestleMania VIII* match and relieved him of the WWF Title.

WWF ANNUAL · 17

BRITISH BULLDOG*

The nemesis of the British Bulldog over the past year was Ric Flair. He pinned the gritty Englishman in the *Survivor Series* after a cheap shot to the back. Flair also eliminated the Bulldog from the *Royal Rumble.*

Other than those two incidents, the Bulldog had a wondrously successful year. Last December, he whipped the massive Warlord after trapping him in a flying cru-

cifix. He wowed the home crowds when European tours took him to his native United Kingdom. "It's the thrill of my life to go back home," he says. And then at *WrestleMania VIII,* he took on the huge Berzerker.

Fans in the UK say that watching the British Bulldog wrestle is the thrill of their lives as well. He can count on their support and loyalty through thick and thin.

SHAWN MICHAELS

*

Fans used to love Shawn Michaels. Most don't anymore. Shawn has become totally full of himself, cocky and self-centered. He says that he has always been greedy for fame and power, although it never showed before. Now Shawn has let it be known he will do anything—no matter how low—to win. Of course, his new manager, who idolizes this pretty boy, encourages him. She is none other than Sensational Sherri.

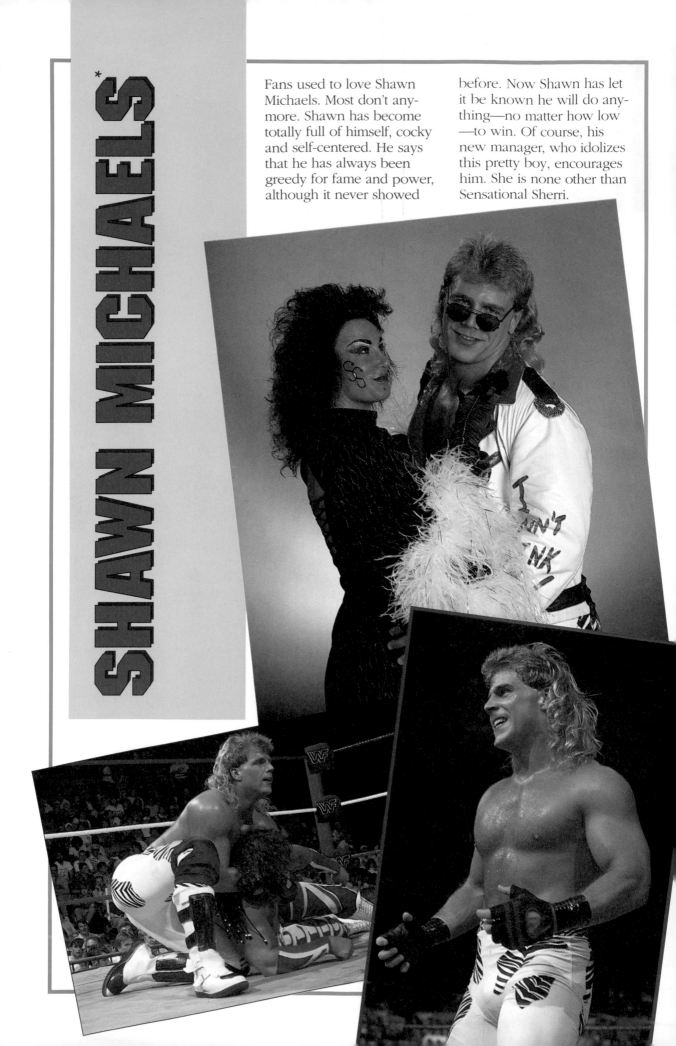

The Man of WrestleMania*

Hulk Hogan is no stranger to *WrestleMania*. He's appeared at every one, including *WrestleMania VIII* this past spring. Below is a little background on Hulk's first seven *WrestleMania* appearances. Can you figure out which is which?

- Hulk fought behind bars at *WrestleMania* __.

- Hulk appeared before the largest audience ever for an indoor sporting event at *WrestleMania* __.

- Hulk lost his title at *WrestleMania* __.

- The Hulkster won the WWF Championship for an unprecedented third time at *WrestleMania* __.

- Hulk had a partner for the only time at *WrestleMania* __.

- Hulk and his opponent were disqualified at *WrestleMania* __.

- The Mega-Powers exploded at *WrestleMania* __.

SID JUSTICE *

There is no such thing as real justice when it comes to Sid Justice. Sid, you see, has proved himself to be a turncoat. Although Hulk Hogan had counted on him as a friend, he ruined the Hulkster's chance to reclaim the WWF Title at the *Royal Rumble*. Then Sid turned against Hulk, taunting and bad-mouthing him. Finally, the two of them met at *WrestleMania VIII*.

The match was titanic. When master of voodoo Papa Shango helped Justice attack Hogan, the Hulkster won via disqualification.

Sid also took on a manager, Harvey Wippleman. Harvey is one of those wormy little guys who like to start fights and then let someone else—in this case, Sid—do the slugging. So Harvey goes out of his way to antagonize Sid Justice's opponents, and then he lets him clean house.

THE ULTIMATE WARRIOR*

The Ultimate Warrior came back to the WWF at *Wrestle-Mania VIII* in a typically explosive style. Hulk Hogan, at the end of his match with Sid Justice, was under heavy assault by Justice and Papa Shango, who had interfered. At this point, the Hulkster was in serious trouble.

Suddenly, from out of the blue, the Ultimate Warrior appeared. Roaring down the aisle toward the ring, the Warrior went at Justice and Shango in a frenzy. His intervention in the match gave Hogan a respite, and the two of them cleared the ring of their adversaries.

Now the Warrior and Papa Shango have a conflict underway. The Warrior says that he will pull out all the stops when he goes up against the voodoo priest in the squared circle. "I will be the one," howls the Warrior, "who will rid the WWF of Papa Shango!"

TATANKA*

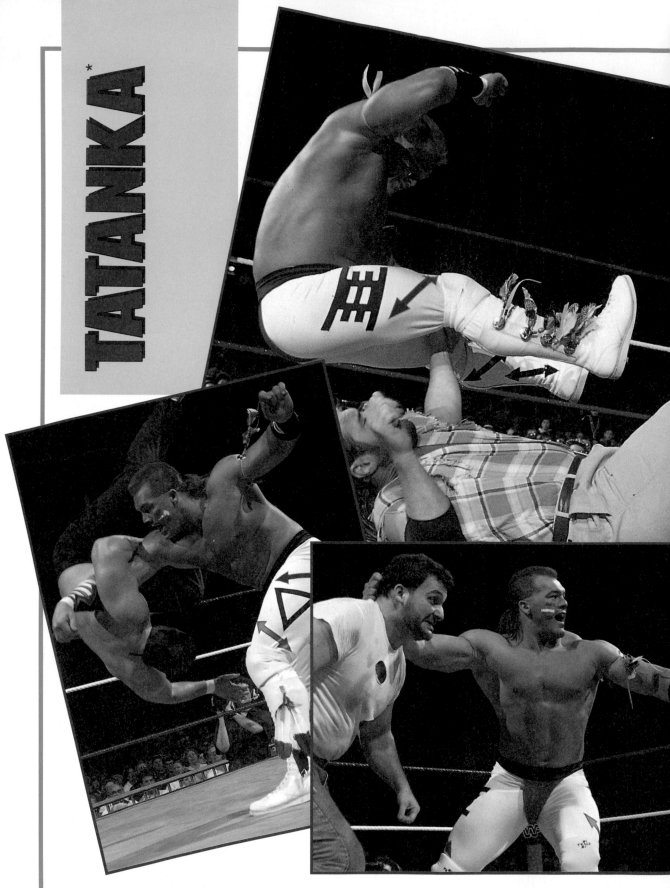

Tatanka, who came to the WWF this year, has people excited. This young member of the Lumbee tribe of Native Americans exudes courage, strength and great athletic ability. He stood out in football, track and other high school and collegiate sports and then made a name for himself as a body-builder. Now it is time to do the same in the WWF.

There is another fascinating aspect to Tatanka. He is

proud of his heritage, and he is the leader of the New Indian Nation. What that means, says Tatanka, is the revival of the traditional values and the spirit of Native Americans.

"We must instill in ourselves our ancestors' love for the environment, their loyalty and courage," he says. "These are the values of the New Indian Nation."

At *WrestleMania VIII*, Tatanka faced the Model and showed considerable mettle by taking on and beating the veteran.

THE NASTY BOYS *

Knobbs and Sags, the Nasty Boys, behave like vicious hoodlums. They are egged on by their manager, Jimmy "Mouth of the South" Hart. They enjoy beating up on their opponents. If someone goes down while in the ring with the Nasty Boys, he will be stomped to jelly. There's no doubt about it.

Most fans loved it when, at *SummerSlam*, the Nastys lost their precious WWF Tag Team Title to the Legion of Doom. The Legion handed Knobbs and Sags a taste of their own medicine.

Later, the Nasty Boys ended up survivors in their *Survivor Series* match. Then, at *WrestleMania VIII*, the Nastys teamed with Repo Man and the Mountie versus Hacksaw Jim Duggan, Sgt. Slaughter, the Big Boss Man and Virgil. The Nasty Boys ended up on the losing side in that battle.

RAMP

Your exclusive WWF knockout tour of the wildest events yet!

This past spring, superstars of the World Wrestling Federation rampaged throughout Europe, bringing wrestling extravaganzas to the United Kingdom, Spain and Italy. Fans in those nations were given the opportunity to see the most talented WWF superstars wage feverish combat between the ring ropes. The British Bulldog, a fan favorite, was on hand for these events, as were psychotic Sid Justice and the awesome Undertaker.

RAMPAGE!

EUROPEAN RAMPAGE AGAIN TOUR

WF   WF   WEMBLEY ARENA

BRITISH BULLDOG

The WWF made several stops in the British Isles and Ireland. Fans in Belfast, Dublin, Birmingham and Glasgow were treated to WWF excitement. The fans at Wembley Arena had two opportunities to catch WWF action and see top-quality matches, such as the Bushwhackers vs. Brooklyn Brawler and IRS. The Model went up against Texas Tornado. The Bulldog and Sgt. Slaughter were also on hand.

Trivia Teasers

It's time for a little WWF trivia. There are five categories of questions, each made up of three questions.

Award yourself one point for answering the first question in each category, two points for answering the second and three points for the third question, the most difficult.

A perfect score is 30, but consider yourself an expert on the WWF if you get as many as 25 points. Between 20-25 is pretty impressive, too. If you get less than 10, maybe you should study up a little.

HEY, BULLDOG

1. What action-packed event did the British Bulldog win during the WWF's last London visit?
2. Do you know what English city is home to the Bulldog?
3. Finally, the Bulldog has repeatedly said that his goal is to be the WWF's what?

HISTORY LESSONS

1. The first *WrestleMania* was held in 1983, '85 or '86?
2. What American television star competed at *WrestleMania I* and *2*?
3. At which *WrestleMania* did the belt **not** change hands?

BY ANY OTHER NAME

1. Who now goes by the nickname "Slick"?
2. Who's the "Eighth Wonder of the World"?
3. What is Owen Hart's nickname?

ON THE ROAD AGAIN

1. What famous London hall was a stop on the WWF's last European Tour?
2. The WWF also visited what Spanish city, site of the 1992 Summer Olympics?
3. Can you name the two other countries that completed the WWF's tour of Europe?

THE PIPES ARE CALLING

1. Rowdy Roddy Piper likes to say when he's good, he's good and when he's bad, he's what?
2. Piper wasn't in the best of health when he appeared with Virgil at *WrestleMania VII*. In fact, he had to use what to make it to ringside?
3. Rowdy Roddy has appeared in a number of films. One was a horror flick directed by John Carpenter. What was the film's title?

BIG BOSS MAN

If there is anything the Big Boss Man dislikes as much as criminals, it's a law enforcer gone bad. And there is one of them in the WWF—the Mountie. They were bound to tangle.

The Mountie started it by a sneak attack in which he zapped the Big Boss Man with his electric cattle prod. Eventually, at *SummerSlam*, they battled in a match in which the loser would end up spending the night in jail. And that's where the Mountie spent his night.

MONEY INC.

The Million Dollar Man Ted DiBiase and IRS, also known as Irwin R. Schyster, knew what they were doing when they joined forces as Money Inc. They obtained Jimmy "Mouth of the South" Hart as their manager, got a match with the WWF Tag Team titlists, Legion of Doom, and took the belts.

Left in the lurch was the team Hart abandoned, the Natural Disasters, who were in line for a title shot. Hart cheated them out of it, instead opting for the big bucks of the Million Dollar Man Ted DiBiase.

"Money talks," DiBiase says of the deal. "And I've got all the money in the world. Ha. Ha. Ha."

Money Inc. lost to the Disasters at *WrestleMania VIII,* but as the victory was by count-out, the Disasters did not win the title.

BRET "HIT MAN" HART*

Bret "Hit Man" Hart courageously risked his WWF Intercontinental Title against the Mountie by wrestling with a high fever. The Hit Man lost. Before he could get a rematch, Rowdy Roddy Piper whipped the Mountie and took the belt.

A match between Piper and Bret was signed for *WrestleMania VIII*. At first Piper did not want to wrestle his friend, Bret, but Piper wouldn't forfeit the title, either. So he and Bret clashed at *WrestleMania VIII* where Bret recaptured his championship belt.

THE BEVERLY BROTHERS *

From the time they were little boys, the parents of the Beverly Brothers, Beau and Blake, spoiled them rotten. They were given anything they wanted. This may be why the Beverly Brothers are so vicious in the WWF ring. You see, in the ring they can't get what they want just by demanding it. They must fight for it. If victory doesn't come right away, the Beverly Brothers get mean and start backstabbing.

The presence of the Genius as manager of the Beverly Brothers makes them even more malicious in the squared circle. The Genius con- cocts all sorts of underhanded plots to help the Beverly Brothers triumph. Thus far, he has been pretty successful in their behalf.

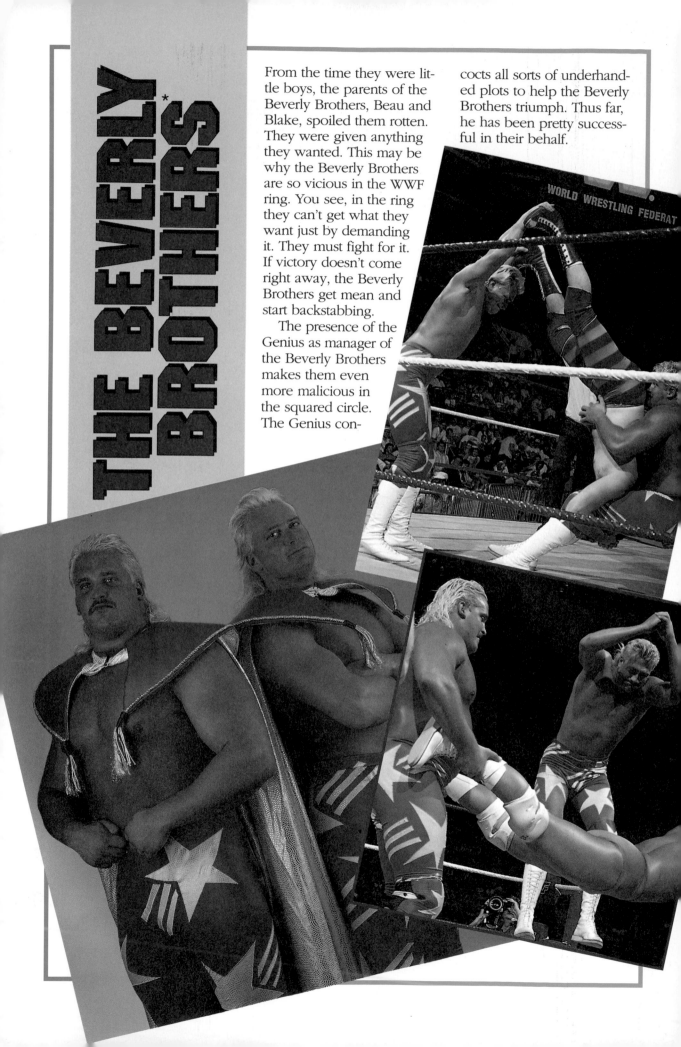

WWF* Word Find

Hidden in the maze of letters are some popular WWF finishing moves. They are (in alphabetical order) the **BIG SPLASH, BOSTON CRAB, CAMEL CLUTCH, CLOTHESLINE, ELBOW SMASH, FULL NELSON, LEGLOCK, PILEDRIVER, POWERSLAM** and **SLEEPERHOLD**. All the words we're after read either across or down. Be careful, though, because some of the words are backward.

A couple of the words overlap. Take the overlapping letters and unscramble them to come up with the following answer: **What is the legendary Hulk Hogan's trademark finisher?** Good luck!

```
B  L  D  G  P  S  S  F  G  U  J  K  L  V  N
E  L  B  O  W  S  M  A  S  H  D  F  B  H  O
C  V  E  J  X  Z  L  D  W  Q  Y  S  I  J  S
P  C  S  Q  S  W  D  Y  K  C  O  L  G  E  L
G  T  U  J  L  B  N  T  G  K  P  W  S  Y  E
M  C  A  M  E  L  C  L  U  T  C  H  P  U  N
A  Q  N  B  E  G  K  B  X  T  Q  V  L  X  L
L  J  U  R  P  D  W  Q  A  K  R  Z  A  D  L
S  C  F  H  E  T  C  Z  V  B  Q  R  S  J  U
R  G  B  A  R  C  N  O  T  S  O  B  H  L  F
E  K  R  V  H  C  S  Y  V  X  M  N  Q  E  Q
W  L  C  L  O  T  H  E  S  L  I  N  E  Z  A
O  T  H  X  L  P  P  J  B  C  Z  P  Y  D  Y
P  I  L  E  D  R  I  V  E  R  C  Q  S  L  K
M  D  D  X  Q  S  G  D  B  H  X  N  M  D  A
```

Legdrop

Gather round
most uniqu
MA

he table with eight of WWF's
ndividuals. They are the wily
NAGERS

As a special feature of our second annual, we invited some of the WWF's managers and consultants to comment on issues they felt were important. We think you'll find their comments interesting. So here are Bobby "The Brain" Heenan, Jimmy "Mouth of the South" Hart, Mr. Perfect, Sensational Sherri, Paul Bearer, Harvey Wippleman, Mr. Fuji and the Genius.

MANAGERS

HEENAN: As the world's best broadcast journalist, I'd like to say I'm amazed at the sad state of affairs in the UK. I used to think you people had some class. No more. London's a dump. Your automobiles should be made in Japan. And the stuff you call food—yuck.

HART: Bobby, they did have the Beatles. Anyway, baby, I want to talk about my tag teams, the Nasty Boys and Money Inc. They're like a one-two punch, daddy. Nobody's better. As for the Natural Disasters, that's just what they are—as disasters, they're naturals.

MR. PERFECT: I'm not exactly a manager, but I'm Executive Consultant to Ric Flair. And all I've got to say is that Ric and I work perfectly together.

SENSATIONAL SHERRI: Let me tell you about my Shawn. He's the best-looking...

PAUL BEARER (interrupting): Yesss, he'd look good in a coffin.

HARVEY WIPPLEMAN: Sid Justice and me, we're the two toughest guys in the WWF. Anybody wants to take us on, we'll kick butt.

MR. FUJI: Fuji like everyone to know he always interested

in managing new wrestlers. But they must stand pain. Lots of pain.

THE GENIUS: Let me tell you something just between us. The best manager in the WWF is the Genius.

The comment by the Genius provoked a frenzied discussion among the managers.

At that point, we decided to end the interview.

THE NATURAL DISASTERS *

Something good happened to the Earthquake and Typhoon of the Natural Disasters this past year. They rid themselves of the unsavory influence of manager Jimmy "Mouth of the South" Hart. He ditched them for the chance to get Money Inc. the WWF Tag Team Title. The Disasters chased Money Inc. from the ring at *WrestleMania VIII* but did not win the title because of the fact the victory was by count-out.

Now the Disasters are ready to set things straight between themselves and Hart and his Money Inc.— the Million Dollar Man Ted DiBiase and IRS. That trio makes a formidable enemy. On the other hand, Earthquake and Typhoon are the two biggest wrestlers in the WWF. In fact, they are positively humongous.

"We are going to hit the Million Dollar Man, IRS and Jimmy Hart so hard their parts are gonna get mixed up," says Earthquake.

"Money Inc.," threatens Typhoon, "the ground is gonna shake, the wind is gonna howl and then you will be blown away."

Certainly, the Disasters have the capability to back up their words with action. Typhoon and Earthquake could use a variety of punishing tactics to bring down Money Inc. If they do, the Disasters will be the biggest WWF Tag Team Champions of all time.

PAPA SHANGO

*

Someone very strange came to the WWF during the year. He's the voodoo man, Papa Shango. This massive and brooding creature of a man is a voodoo priest, who enjoys using the darker side of voodoo to plot against his foes. He also uses a smashing shoulderbreaker to destroy his adversaries.

Papa Shango's origins are mysterious. Just where he mastered his black art is not known. What is known, however, is that he plans to conjure and batter his way to the top of the WWF. In the squared circle thus far, Shango has demonstrated fearsome force and the will to pull out all the stops. He disregards the orders of the referee until the last possible moment, leaving his opponents dazed and wobbly from his illegal blows.

"I will turn my opponents into zombies," warns Papa Shango. "They will have no minds of their own. Their minds will be ruled by one man—Papa Shango."

Papa Shango has battled many superstars, including the Undertaker. Shango says that he will cast an evil spell over the Pale Destroyer and his manager. Papa Shango is a dangerous foe, and he has instilled fear in the hearts of many WWF superstars.

THE ROCKET OWEN HART*

The younger brother of Bret "Hit Man" Hart, Owen Hart is earning a reputation for being one of the most coordinated and agile athletes in the WWF. Opponents who try to sling him around the ring find that he almost always lands on his feet. And opponents who attempt to throw him over the ropes find that he bounces right back at them. He flies into the air with abandon, striking with endless aerial tactics. The Rocket is a great nickname for him.

Scrambled Cities

A number of American cities have hosted *WrestleMania*. Five are scrambled below. It's up to you to unscramble them.

G C A H C I O _ _ _ _ _ _ ☐

W N E   K R O Y ☐ _ _ _ _ ☐ _

S L O   G L E A E S N _ ☐ _ _ _ _ _ _ _ _

D S I N N A L I P O I A _ _ _ _ _ _ _ _ ☐ _ _ _

T A L I C T A N   Y T I C _ ☐ _ _ _ _ _ _ _ ☐ _

You're not finished yet, though. Now, take the letters in the boxes and unscramble them to answer the question.
What's the only city outside the U.S. to host WrestleMania?
It's _ _ _ _ _ _ _ _.

WRESTLEM[

Macho Man Randy Savage, raging at the earlier insults to his wife, Elizabeth, by WWF Champion Ric Flair, gained his revenge at *WrestleMania VIII*. Savage beat Flair and won the title, the second time he has held it. The Immortal Hulk Hogan wrestled what was reported to be his last match in the WWF. Bret "Hit Man" Hart beat Rowdy Roddy Piper for the WWF Intercontinental Title.

The Hoosier Dome in Indianapolis, Indiana, shook with thunder as Savage and Flair tangled. Savage was incensed over the doctored photos earlier provided by Flair to *WWF Magazine*. They seemed to show Elizabeth hanging out with Flair before meeting Savage. The Macho Man took the battle to Flair, but Flair eventually used a foreign object and interference by his consultant, Mr. Perfect, to hurt Savage badly. In the end, however, Savage—with the help of a handful of tights—scored a comeback pin and won the title.

Hogan almost had the massive Sid Justice ready for defeat when manager Harvey Wippleman and the brutal Papa Shango interfered. As Justice and Shango beat up Hogan, the Ultimate Warrior suddenly exploded down the aisle and came to the rescue of Hogan,

who was awarded the win by disqualification. If the match indeed was the Hulkster's last, it was fitting that he and the Warrior should have been reunited, as they were in mid-ring.

Bret "Hit Man" Hart and WWF Intercontinental Champion Rowdy Roddy Piper fought as if they had not been long-time friends. Fists flew amid all-out brawling and solid wrestling. When Hart won, Piper graciously handed him the belt, and they left the ring together. Money Inc., the Million Dollar Man Ted DiBiase and IRS, held onto the tag team title against the Natural Disasters, Earthquake and Typhoon, but only by quitting and losing via count-out, which cannot cause a title to change hands. The Disasters tossed their smaller foes around like dolls, prompting Money Inc. to run for cover.

After surviving two DDTs by Jake "The Snake" Roberts, the Undertaker crushed the Snake with a Tombstone reverse piledriver and pinned him. Again the Undertaker proved he is almost impossible to hurt. It was an awesome performance for the Pale Destroyer of the WWF. The Big Boss Man, Sgt. Slaughter, Hacksaw Jim Duggan and Virgil teamed against the Nasty Boys, Mountie and Repo Man. Virgil scored the pin for his team over Nasty Boy Knobbs.

El Matador pounded the Sexy Boy, Shawn Michaels, almost to a pulp until Michaels began using illegal tactics and beat his opponent. Young Tatanka, the dazzling Native American of the Lumbee Indian tribe, took on vicious veteran the Model Rick Martel. Tatanka showed his stuff by ambushing Rick Martel and scoring the pin.

Another new sensation in the WWF, the Rocket Owen Hart, matched wits and brawn with Skinner. The Rocket used his agility and wrestling skill to overcome Skinner—a great showing for the youngster.

Wrestle With Words

ACROSS

1. Rowdy Roddy Piper's hometown (7)
4. Piper's countrymen (5)
7. Throw out (4)
8. Strength (8)
10. *WrestleMania VII* site (3,7)
12. Root for (5)
13. A country visited by the WWF on its last European Tour (5)
14. What the "F" in WWF stands for (10)
18. Rocker Ozzy Osbourne was in attendance when the British _____ captured the WWF Tag Team Title at *WrestleMania 2* (8)
19. Kick (4)
20. The Macho Man's real first name (5)
21. Worked out in preparation for a bout (7)

DOWN

1. Snarl (5)
2. Helped (8)
3. What Elizabeth wore on her wedding day (5)
4. At what WWF event did Liz tie the knot (10)
5. The *Royal Rumble* is an _____-the-top battle royal (4)
6. Keep from falling (7)
9. Hostile (10)
11. Hulk hails from Venice Beach, _____ia (8)
12. Beat badly (7)
15. Indianapolis' Hoosier Dome was the site of this *WrestleMania* (5)
16. Renowned (5)
17. Proud American Hacksaw Jim Duggan makes his home in _____s Falls, New York (4)

THE MOUNTIE *

"I am the Mountie." It's a saying, it's a song, and it's the motto of the Mountie. He claims to be a law enforcer, but in reality he practices police brutality.

A few months ago, the Mountie held the WWF Intercontinental Title. He took it from a fever-stricken Bret Hart. The Mountie was riding high after this feat. His joy didn't last long. A short time later, Rowdy Roddy Piper tangled with the Mountie and relieved him of his title.

HACKSAW JIM DUGGAN * SGT. SLAUGHTER *

Some people call these two rugged patriots "America's Team." Last summer, however, Sgt. Slaughter was a bitter opponent of his own country, a supporter of dictators. After a *SummerSlam* defeat, he retired into hiding. But then a transformation occurred. He regained his love of country and cast aside his former allies.

Duggan is a perfect partner for Slaughter. For both, it's: "My country—right or wrong." Also their wrestling styles match. No fancy stuff, just get in there and fight the good fight. They are a credit to the land they love.

REPO MAN

*

A repo man is a fellow who repossesses automobiles whose owners have failed to make payments on them. Repo men often strike at night, when their victims are unaware they are around. That's how the WWF's Repo Man acts in the ring. He slinks around, waiting for his opponent to lose focus on him. Then he strikes. Once the opponent is beaten, Repo trusses him on a tow rope and makes his repossession.

Puzzle Answers

Scrambled Cities

The Scrambled Cities are CHICAG**O**, **N**EW YORK, **L**OS ANGELES, INDIANAPO-LIS and A**T**LANTIC CITY. The only city outside the U.S. to host *WrestleMania* is **TORONTO**.

The Man of WrestleMania

The *WrestleManias* are, from top to bottom, 2, III, VI, VII, I, IV and V.

Trivia Teasers

HEY, BULLDOG, the battle royal, Leeds, and greatest British superstar; **HISTORY LESSONS**, 1985, Mr. T, and *WrestleMania III*; **BY ANY OTHER NAME**, Ric Flair, Andre the Giant, and the Rocket; **ON THE ROAD AGAIN**, Royal Albert Hall, Barcelona, and France and Belgium; **THE PIPES ARE CALLING**, he's better, crutches, and *They Live*.

How'd you do?

WWF Word Find

```
B L D G P S S F G U J K L V N
E L B O W S M A S H D F B H O
C V E J X Z L D W Q Y S I J S
P C S Q S W D Y K C O L G E L
G T U J L B N T G K P W S Y E
M C A M E L C L U T C H P U N
A Q N B E G K B X T Q V L X L
L J U R P D W Q A K R Z A D L
S C F H E T C Z V B Q R S J U
R G B A R C N O T S O B H L F
E K R V H C S Y V X M N Q E Q
W L C L O T H E S L I N E Z A
O T H X L P P J B C Z P Y D Y
P I L E D R I V E R C Q S L K
M D D X Q S G D B H X N M D A
```

Hulk's trademark finisher is the **LEGDROP**.

Wrestle With Words

```
 G L A S G O W   S C O T S
 R   S   H   U   V   U
 O U S T   F I R M N E S S
 W   I   U   T   M   R
 L O S A N G E L E S     T
     T   F     R   C   A
 C H E E R   S P A I N  I
 L   D   I   L   L   N
 O   F E D E R A T I O N
 B   G N I M   F   O
 B U L L D O G S   B O O T
 E   E L   H     R   E
 R A N D Y   T R A I N E D
```

THE BUSHWHACKERS*

The Bushwhackers, cousins Luke and Butch, inspire affection in all of their fans. Basically, it is because the Bushwhackers are wild and crazy guys. They get lots of laughs out of life, and their nutty antics always make people happy.

That is, except for their opponents. No one knows what to expect when Luke and Butch enter the ring. It is almost impossible for foes to plan ahead against them. So Luke and Butch go on their rollicking way—and go on winning matches.